Love
each Other

1 JOHN

New Community Bible Study Series

JOHN ORTBERG

WITH KEVIN **&** SHERRY HARNEY

New Community
KNOWING. LOVING. SERVING. CELEBRATING.

Love each Other

I JOHN

WILLOW
Willow Creek Resources

ZONDERVAN™

GRAND RAPIDS, MICHIGAN 49530 USA

1 John: Love Each Other
Copyright © 1999 by the Willow Creek Association

Requests for information should be addressed to:

▦ ZondervanPublishingHouse
Grand Rapids, Michigan 49530

ISBN: 0-310-22768-2

Interior design by Sherri Hoffman

Printed in the United States of America

05 06 07 /❖ EP/ 15 14 13 12 11 10 9

CONTENTS

God has created us for community. This need is built into the very fiber of our being, the DNA of our spirit. As Christians, our deepest desire is to see the truth of God's Word as it influences our relationship with others. We long for a dynamic encounter with God's Word, intimate closeness with His people, and radical transformation of our lives. But how can we accomplish those three difficult tasks?

The New Community Bible Study Series creates a place for all of this to happen. In-depth Bible study, community-building opportunities, and life-changing applications are all built into every session of this small group study guide.

How to Build Community

How do we build a strong, healthy Christian community? The whole concept for this study grows out of a fundamental understanding of Christian community that is dynamic and transformational. We believe that Christians don't simply gather to exchange doctrinal affirmations. Rather, believers are called by God to get into each other's lives. We are family, for better or for worse, and we need to connect with each other.

Community is not built through sitting in the same building and singing the same songs. It is forged in the fires of life. When we know each other deeply—the good, the bad, and the ugly—community is experienced. Community grows when we learn to rejoice with one another, celebrating life. Roots grow deep when we know we are loved by others and are free to extend love to them as well. Finally, community deepens and is built when we commit to serve each other and let others serve us. This process of doing ministry and humbly receiving the ministry of others is critical for healthy community life.

Build Community Through Knowing and Being Known

We all long to know others deeply and to be fully known by them. Although we might run from this level of intimacy at times, we all want to have people in our lives who trust us enough to disclose the deep and tender parts of themselves. In turn, we want to reveal some of our feelings, expressing them freely to people we trust.

The first section of each of these six studies creates a place for deep knowing and being known. Through serious reflection on the truth of Scripture, you will be invited to communicate parts of your heart and life with your small group members. You might even discover yourself opening parts of your heart that you have thus far kept hidden. The Bible study and discussion questions do not encourage surface conversation. The only way to go deep in knowing others and being known by them is to dig deep, and this takes some work. Knowing others also takes trust—that you will honor each other and respect each other's confidences.

Build Community Through Celebrating and Being Celebrated

If you have not had a good blush recently, read a short book in the Bible called Song of Songs. It's a record of a bride and groom writing poetic and romantic love letters to each other. They are freely celebrating every conceivable aspect of each other's personality, character, and physical appearance. At one point the groom says, "You have made my heart beat fast with a single glance from your eyes." Song of Songs is a reckless celebration of life, love, and all that is good.

We need to recapture the joy and freedom of celebration. In every session of this study, your group will commit to celebrate together. Although there are many ways to express joy, we will let our expression of celebration come through prayer. In each session you will take time to come before the God of joy and celebrate who He is and what He is doing. You will also have opportunity to celebrate what God is doing in your life and the lives of those who are a part of your small group. You will become a community of affirmation, celebration, and joy through your prayer time together.

You will need to be sensitive during this time of prayer together. Not everyone feels comfortable praying with a group of people. Be aware that each person is starting at a different place in their freedom to pray in a group, and be patient. Seek to promote a warm and welcoming atmosphere where each person can stretch a little and learn what it means to be a community that celebrates with God in the center.

Build Community Through Loving and Being Loved

Unless we are exchanging deeply committed levels of love with a few people, we will die slowly on the inside. This is precisely why so many people feel almost nothing at all. If we don't learn to exchange love with family and friends, we will eventually grow numb and no longer believe love is even a possibility. This is not God's plan. He hungers for us to be loved and to give love to others. As a matter of fact, He wants this for us even more than we want it for ourselves.

Every session in this study will address the area of loving and being loved. You will be challenged, in your personal life and as a small group, to be intentional and consistent about building love relationships. You will get practical tools and be encouraged to set measurable goals for giving and receiving love.

Build Community Through Serving and Being Served

Community is about serving and humbly allowing others to serve you. The single most stirring example of this is recorded in John 13, where Jesus takes the position of the lowest servant and washes the feet of His followers. He gives them a powerful example and then calls them to follow. Servanthood is at the very core of community. To sustain deep relationships over a long period of time, there must be humility and a willingness to serve each other.

At the close of each session will be a clear challenge to servanthood. As a group, and as individual followers of Christ, you will discover that community is built through serving others. You will also find that your own small group members will grow in their ability to extend service to your life.

Bible Study Basics

To get the most out of this study, you will need to prepare and participate. Here are some guidelines to help you.

Preparing for the Study

1. If possible, even if you are not the leader, look over each lesson before you meet, read the Bible passages, and answer the questions. The more you are prepared, the more you will gain from the study.
2. Begin your preparation time with prayer. Ask God to help you understand the passage and apply it to your life.
3. A good modern translation, such as the New International Version, the New American Standard Bible, or the New Revised Standard Version, will give you the most help. Questions in this guide are based on the New International Version.
4. Read and reread the passages. You must know what the passage says before you can understand what it means and how it applies to you.
5. Write your answers in the spaces provided in the study guide. This will help you to participate more fully in the discussion and will also help you personalize what you are learning.
6. Keep a Bible dictionary handy to look up unfamiliar words, names, or places.

Participating in the Study

1. Be willing to join in the discussion. The leader of the group will not be lecturing but will encourage people to discuss what they have learned in the passage. Plan to share what God has taught you during your preparation time.
2. Stick to the passages being studied. Base your answers on the verses being discussed rather than on outside authorities such as commentaries or your favorite author or speaker.

3. Try to be sensitive to the other members of the group. Listen attentively when they speak, and be affirming whenever you can. This will encourage more hesitant members of the group to participate.
4. Be careful not to dominate the discussion. By all means participate, but allow others to have equal time.
5. If you are a discussion leader or a participant who wants further insights, you will find additional comments in the Leader's Notes at the back of this book.

1 John: Love Each Other

Have you ever wondered if God really loves you? If you are confident that God loves you, have you ever wondered why? Do you ever struggle with sin and wish you had greater power to resist and overcome it? Have you ever longed to experience God's forgiveness and love on a more profound level? Do you desire to deepen your love for people and want to discover how to receive their love more freely?

If you answered any of these questions with a yes, the book of 1 John is for you. These were the very issues facing the followers of Christ that John addresses in this power-packed letter. They needed to know God's love in new and fresh ways. They longed for overcoming power to be unleashed in their lives. Their hearts hungered to know God's forgiveness in all its fullness. And these Christians desired to express love and receive it with others in the family of God, as well as those who were still outside of the family.

In the midst of their worry, fear, and doubt, John wrote to bring assurance, hope, and confidence. John's readers found direction in this life-changing letter. And so will you!

A Crisis of Faith

In the latter part of the first century numerous congregations sprang up primarily through the teachings of the apostle John. Many of them were in Asia Minor, where the people met regularly for worship in house churches. Some of these congregations had been around for decades, but now they were facing a very trying time in their faith.

These Christians were at a crisis point because false teachers were casting a shadow of doubt over their faith. These deceptive teachers claimed to have special knowledge from God and about God. They claimed that *only* those who followed their very narrow teaching belonged to God. The problem was, what they were teaching did not fit with the gospel that John had written.

This caused confusion and uncertainty for these congregations of believers. They were hanging by a thread because of the false teaching they were hearing. As a matter of fact, some of these young Christians were beginning to be confused about even the most basic teachings of the faith. In response to this turmoil, John wrote a clear and powerful letter which called the early Christians back to the basics of their faith. He reminded them of the bedrock foundational teachings that Christians in every century need to remember.

An Invitation to Love

John does not write about abstract ideas on the periphery of life. He gets to the heart of the matter. This letter was the desperate attempt of a father to anchor his children securely in the faith. The topics John addresses in this book get right at the core of what it means to live as children of God. In the middle of it all is love:

> Dear friends, let us love one another, for love comes from God. Everyone who loves has been born of God and knows God. Whoever does not love does not know God, because God is love. This is how God showed his love among us: He sent his one and only Son into the world that we might live through him. This is love: not that we loved God, but that he loved us and sent his Son as an atoning sacrifice for our sins. Dear friends, since God so loved us, we also ought to love one another. No one has ever seen God; but if we love one another, God lives in us and his love is made complete in us.

> (1 John 4:7–12)

Our spiritual confidence, hope, power to overcome, forgiveness of sin, and direction for life all begin and end with the love of God. John calls us back to the basics of faith. God's love for us, our love for God, and our love for one another.

John's invitation is a call to walk in love. This is an invitation each one of us needs to hear over and over again. My prayer is that you will not only hear this invitation, but that you will accept it. If you do, your life will never be the same.

It's a Sin Thing

I JOHN 1:5–2:2

Have you ever heard the phrase, "It's a God thing"? When something amazing happens, we exclaim, "It's a God thing!" When a prayer is answered in a clear and undeniable way, we declare, "It's a God thing!" When worship is invaded by the powerful and life-changing presence of the Spirit of God, we proclaim, "It's a God thing!" When a hardened sinner falls to his knees and surrenders to Christ, we agree, "It's a God thing!"

There is no other way to account for it! The fingerprints of God are all over these experiences, so we say, "It's a God thing!" Since hearing this phrase, I have willingly adopted it, because it expresses so much in so few words.

When we say this, there is no intention of being irreverent. We are simply saying God is real, active, and present right where we live. "It's a God thing" is a way to express what we have all experienced at one time or another. Our whole faith is built on the understanding that God works in human history. The ultimate "God thing" was the coming of Jesus Christ into the world and our lives.

But there is another phrase that needs to enter our language. It is not as much fun, but it is just as important. As a matter of fact, if we hope to say, "It's a God thing" often, we will need to first learn to say this other phrase. It has to do with our willingness to face up to the fact that there is darkness in us still. The phrase we must learn to speak is, "It's a sin thing!"

When we speak these words, "It's a sin thing!" we don't do so in accusation of others. Rather, it is a confessional statement all of us followers of Christ need to speak of ourselves. We take honest inventory, see our hearts and lives as they really are, and admit that the "sin thing" still has a grip on us. We need to admit that we still struggle with the lure, influence, and power of sin in our lives.

Making the Connection

1. What is one "God thing" you have experienced in the past year?

   How have you seen the "sin thing" at work in your life?

Knowing and Being Known

2. John declares that God is light. What are some of the parallels we can draw between light and God?

3. What is the first claim the false teachers were making about sin (1:6)?

Facing False Claims

In this first chapter, John identifies three false claims about sin. These claims always begin with the words, "If we claim ..." These deceptive claims were being lifted up by false teachers who were seeking to infect others with their erroneous understanding of sin. After identifying each false claim, John draws out some of the implications of this misunderstanding. Then John corrects the false teaching with the truth. He directs us to the correct teaching by using the key word *if*. Once we have the correct understanding before us, John draws out the reality of the powerful and life-changing implications of walking in the truth.

It is striking to notice that the false claims made by these deceptive teachers almost two thousand years ago still exist today. Not only are they being propagated by false teachers, but they lurk in the corners of each of our hearts. We need to shed light on these inaccurate views of sin and let the truth be known!

Read 1 John 1:5–7

What did John teach about sin to correct this faulty understanding (1:7)?

4. How have your relationships with others become more authentic since you have confessed your sins and become a follower of Christ?

Look in the Mirror

A prison of pride is filled with self-made men and women determined to pull themselves up by their own bootstraps even if they land on their own rear ends. It does not matter what they did or to whom they did it or where they will end up; it only matters that "I did it my way."

You've seen the prisoners. You've seen the alcoholic who won't admit his drinking problem. You've seen the woman who refuses to talk with anyone about her fears. You've seen the businessman who adamantly rejects help, even when his dreams are falling apart.

Perhaps to see such a prisoner all you have to do is look in the mirror.

—Max Lucado, *The Applause of Heaven* (Word, 1990)

Read 1 John 1:8–9

5. What is the second claim the false teachers were making about sin (1:8)?

What did John teach about sin to correct this false understanding (1:9)?

6. What are some of the traits and characteristics you see in the lives of people who are working overtime to prove to themselves, others, and God, that they are "good people" and not sinful?

How have you experienced freedom and peace when you have admitted your sinfulness to God?

7. John uses very strong words to describe those who have confessed their sins. He says we are "*purified* from *all* unrighteousness." If you are a follower of Christ, describe the way that God sees you, in light of John's teaching.

Read I John 1:10–2:2

8. What is the third claim the false teachers were making about sin (1:10)?

Seeing Sin

The sins we see easiest in others we have learned first in ourselves; we know their behavior and their signs from the inside. Though they deny the personal fault, gossips spot gossips a mile away, as wolves know wolves by a familial scent. Is he neglectful? Impatient? Judgmental? Self-indulgent? Jealous? Scornful? Abusive? So, sometime and somewhere, were you—

Recall: that if you did not commit the sin against your spouse, yet you did, once, against your parents, your adolescent classmates, your friends, your colleagues at work, the teller in the bank, another race, another class of people, the poor. Or you did in your heart what you didn't have the temerity to do openly with your hands.

But recall these sins not to torment yourself, rather to rejoice in the forgiveness God has given you—you personally—since God was always at the other end of your sin, and did not return judgment for iniquity, but mercy.

—Walter Wangerin, Jr., *Measuring the Days* (HarperCollins, 1993)

What do people prove about themselves if they accept this false claim (1:10)?

What is John's message for followers of Christ who do sin (2:1–2)?

9. If Jesus Christ is the final and complete sacrifice for our sins, what would He say to those who feel the need to measure up or do something to "pay for" their sins?

10. Jesus Christ did not just die for "my sins" but for the sins of the whole world. How should this truth influence the way you will conduct yourself in the coming week in one of the following places:

- In your workplace
- In your neighborhood
- In your shops or restaurants
- In your home

Celebrating and Being Celebrated

Take some time as a group to praise God for some of the "God things" you have experienced in your own lives over the past months. Let God know that you see His hand working and that you celebrate His power at work.

Loving and Being Loved

Talk as a group about one member of your church who consistently communicates the love of Jesus to others. He or she could be an up-front kind of leader, or a behind-the-scenes person whom most people don't usually notice. Agree as a group that each of you will drop this person a note or give him or her a personal word of affirmation in the coming week. Extend the love of Christ to this person who has been so faithfully walking in the light.

Serving and Being Served

Jesus did not just die for His followers. He died for all people: "He is the atoning sacrifice for our sins, and not only for ours but also for the sins of the whole world" (1 John 2:2).

If Jesus died for the world, and if God loves the world, we need to be willing to show His love through acts of service and charity. Talk as a group about one practical act of service you can extend to a person or family that does not yet know that Jesus died as the sacrifice for their sins. Contact this person or family and offer the service your group has agreed to extend.

Let your service connect with their life on three levels:

1. Bathe this experience in prayer. Pray that your loving service will show the love of God.
2. Bring your service with hearts filled with joy.
3. If those you serve ask why you have cared for them, let them know that your lives are overwhelmed by the love and grace of God and that you want to extend this to others.

Experiencing God's Forgiveness

I JOHN I:8–2:6

A few years ago, my wife was pulled over by an Illinois law enforcement officer for driving too fast. The officer said to Nancy, "Could I have your license?" He went to his squad car, and after a few minutes came back and said, "This is not an Illinois license; this is a California license. How long have you lived in Illinois?" Nancy answered, "We've lived here for a year and a half." The officer asked her, "Why don't you have an Illinois license?" She explained that for her it is a statement, a protest against the weather in Illinois. It is her personal form of denial that she no longer lives in the Sunshine State.

He then asked her, "Do you have car insurance?" She said, "Sure" and handed it over. After another minute or two at the squad car, he returned and said, "This insurance card is expired! Do you have a new one?" She said, "I'm sure we do, but I think it's at home." He then asked her for a "bond card." She explained that she had never heard of one and had never seen one. He then asked if she had $75 to post, and she informed him that she had no cash. But she did inform him that if you offered a policeman $75 on the side of the road in California, they'd lock you up for a while.

Nancy then informed the policeman that she was an AAA member. He asked her for the card, but she had left it at home because it was a California card. He headed back to his squad car for the third time. When he finally came back, he gave her back her license and said, "Lady, it is more trouble for me to write up this ticket than it is worth. I'm going to let you go with a warning."

Nancy was living in temporary grace. She got off without a penalty, but the officer said, "I'll be watching for you." If you have ever been pulled over, you know how you feel while driving in the following days. There is a sense of fear. In Nancy's case, until all the stuff got cleared up, she lived in fear . . . knowing the hammer *could* have fallen at any moment. She experienced a moment of grace, but not for a lifetime!

Sadly, this is the case for many followers of Christ. They experience a moment of grace, but not a lifetime of grace. They go through life under a cloud. I believe the problem is not a lack of information. I think most Christians have listened to many messages on grace. They hear over and over that God is a gracious God who loves them. We don't need another lesson about grace or more information that God is gracious. What is missing is an indispensable tool for a healthy and authentic spiritual life. I think what is missing is a practice that spiritually wise people have known about for centuries. What we need in the church today is more followers of Christ who really know how to *confess*.

Making the Connection

1. Describe a time when you experienced momentary grace, but knew it would not last. This could be in the workplace, in a friendship, with a law enforcement officer, in your spiritual life, or in any life situation.

Knowing and Being Known

Read I John 1:8–10

2. Why is personal admission of sin essential as the starting point of the confession process?

What happens when we refuse to acknowledge our sin?

Climbing the Mountain of Confession
Step 1—Acknowledge Your Sin

In this study we will look at five aspects of confession. These are like steps up a mountain toward the breathtaking view of God's grace. This discipline of true confession has been practiced by followers of Christ throughout the history of the church.

First, we need to come to the point where we can acknowledge our sins before ourselves, God, and others. Open admission is essential. This does not mean we constantly air our sins and talk about them. Rather, we choose to honestly and humbly admit our battle with sin.

Often we try to cover for ourselves. What begins as a confession ends up being an excuse: "I didn't mean to yell at you; I had a bad day." To confess means to own up to the reality that my behavior is not just the result of bad parenting, poor genes, jealous siblings, or a chemical imbalance from eating too many Twinkies. All of these may be involved, because human behavior is complex, but confession is about saying that somewhere in that mix was a choice of my will. That choice was made by me. And it does not need to be excused, explained, or understood, but forgiven!

3. Tell about a time from your childhood when you tried to hide something you did wrong from your parents and finally admitted what you had done.

What happened in your heart when you finally admitted your wrongdoing?

What happened in your relationship with your parents when you acknowledged what you did?

Read 1 John 2:1–2

4. John moves us to focus our eyes on the ultimate cost of our sin and the sacrifice that was paid for us. If we are going to have a new way of seeing, we need to look at the cross and see what our sins cost God. When you turn your eyes to the cross, how does this picture impact the way you see your sin?

Climbing the Mountain of Confession
Step 2—See with New Eyes

After acknowledging our sin to God, ourselves, and others, we need to learn to see our sin with new eyes. We need to learn to see how our sin looks through the eyes of the people we have sinned against. How has our sin hurt them, and what has it done to them? Also, we begin to see our sin through the eyes of God. How have we hurt God?

Jesus often spoke about the need for this kind of perspective. He said, "How can you say to your brother, 'Let me take the speck out of your eye,' when all the time there is a plank in your own eye? You hypocrite, first take the plank out of your own eye, and then you will see clearly to remove the speck from your brother's eye" (Matthew 7:4–5). Jesus was talking to religious leaders who saw themselves as pretty good people. Proud of their spiritual superiority and in denial about their own behavior, they looked at the sins of prostitutes, cheaters, and tax collectors and refused to be around such sinful undesirables. They needed to take the log out of their own eyes so they could see the truth about their own actions. They needed a new way of seeing life that allowed them to see the cost of their own sins and stop focusing on the sins of everyone else.

5. What causes us to focus so much on the sins of others?

What have you learned that helps you get your eyes off the sins of others and start focusing on your own sins?

Climbing the Mountain of Confession
Step 3—Feel the Pain of the Victim

Confession is not just an exchange of information. It involves entering into the pain of the person you have hurt. It also means entering into God's pain over sin. Confession can bring pain, but it is not the kind of pain that makes you beat yourself up for a long time and exile yourself to the spiritual time-out chair until you are worthy to come back into fellowship with God and others. It involves seeing sin and your life in such a way that you say, "I wish I could take that back; I don't want to be that kind of person. I don't want to do that anymore. I feel that what I have done to God and others hurts them, and I long for the power to change!" That kind of pain is healing and Christ-honoring.

Read James 4:7–10

6. We often tend to see tears and mourning as a sign of weakness. How does James present mourning as healing and redemptive?

7. Describe a time when you realized the pain you caused God, or another person, because of your sin.

How did entering into their pain help you resist this sin in the future?

Read 1 John 2:3–6

8. In light of what John teaches in this passage, what do you think he would say to the person who boldly declares: "I'm truly sorry for my sin and how I hurt others, but I just can't change. This is the way that I am."

9. What is one promise you need to make to God in relationship to an area of sin in your life?

Climbing the Mountain of Confession
Step 4—Promise

When we have acknowledged our sin, seen the damage our sin has done, and felt the pain of God's heart and the pain of others, we discover that our desires begin to change. We no longer want to sin.

When you feel deeply sorrowful about the hurt you caused, you want to change. So you make a promise: "I resolve, with God's help, to change." This may involve making right what you did wrong. It could involve making reparations, as in the story of Zacchaeus (Luke 19). When Zacchaeus met Jesus face-to-face, he was convicted of his own sins of taking more taxes than were required. He had been stealing from people. Upon meeting Jesus, he made a promise to pay back what he had taken. He promised to make things right!

Climbing the Mountain of Confession
Step 5—Accept Grace

We must remember that our confession is not about trying to gain God's favor or measure up by our human efforts. Confession begins with a profound understanding of grace. The climax of this journey of confession is when we discover that at the top of the mountain of confession is even more grace ... beyond description. When we refuse to confess, we cut ourselves off from the riches of grace God longs for us to experience. When we freely confess our sins, we experience joy, freedom, and power to change. Grace is available to all who are ready to confess their sins.

How can your small group members challenge you and hold you accountable to keep your promise in this area?

10. If confession sets us free to experience such indescribable grace, why are we so slow to confess our sins?

11. How have you experienced the height and depth of God's grace through confession?

What would you say to those who are reluctant to confess their sins?

Celebrating and Being Celebrated

God has given us more than we could ever thank Him for. We know that "every good and perfect gift is from above" (James 1:17). The greatest of all His gifts was His only Son, Jesus Christ. Through Jesus we experience forgiveness of sins and grace beyond measure. Take time as a group to pray together and celebrate the greatest gift ever given and received: Jesus Christ.

Loving and Being Loved

Through the history of the church, followers of Christ have known the power of tears. When we realize how we have hurt another person through our sinful attitudes and actions, we should be moved to tears. If you have hurt someone through a choice you have made, through an action you have taken, or through something you failed to do, go to that person and let him or her know that you grieve over what you have done. If you have wept over this, let that person know. Ask him or her to pray for you as you learn to turn from this kind of sinful behavior and seek to walk in the grace of Christ. This level of humble confession can be one of the greatest actions of love you might ever extend to another person.

Serving and Being Served

We all have the tendency to notice the sliver in the eye of another person while we ignore the log in our own eye. Let your act of service be to release another person from the judgment you have been holding over them. Pray for eyes to see your own sin and not focus on their sins anymore. (This does not mean that you will tell your small group members about another person's sin, but about the condition of your heart while you have been focusing on someone else's sin.) Invite your small group members to pray for you in this process.

If your attitude toward this person begins to change as you stop focusing on the "sliver in their eye," tell your small group about this as an encouragement for all of you to serve through extending grace.

Overcoming the Sin Thing

I JOHN 3:4–10

Often Christians ask questions like:
How much sin can I have in my life before I hit a danger zone?
Are there low levels of sin that are okay before I get to a toxic level?

These are the wrong questions for followers of Christ to ask. The right question is, *Am I growing more and more sensitive and responsive to Jesus in my life?* The real question is directional, *Am I moving toward the light or away from it?* The truth is, it will take some discernment to get the right answer. The questions we need to be asking, when it comes to sin, are directional, not quantitative.

Too often we want to give ourselves a spiritual pat on the back because we are not committing heinous and overtly sinful actions. What we need to remember is that we all start at different points. It might take more courage for a young person growing up in the inner city to walk away from being part of a gang than it would take for another person to give all they own to the poor. Because we all start at different places, we can't quantify our actions. The key question we need to ask is, *Am I moving toward God or away from God?*

If we are going to effectively battle against the "sin thing," we need to recognize that often the most dangerous sins are the subtle and socially acceptable sins. All sin is wrong. And it all produces spiritual death. Scripture is clear about this. But we often view some sins as minor. The very attitudes and actions we secretly label as acceptable can be far more dangerous than we might ever dream.

The best way to assess the damage of a particular sin is to determine the extent to which it separates you from God. How does this attitude or action move you out of the light and into the darkness?

It takes some discernment to work on this. Many people in the church have the attitude, "I don't have major sin in my life. I know that theologically and theoretically I am just as guilty as anyone else, but I don't need a major overhaul, like some people do. All I need is a little tune-up."

Making the Connection

1. What are some of the "big" and "scandalous" sins that most Christ followers agree are wrong?

What are some of the more "acceptable" and "tolerated" sins in our world, and in the church, today?

Going After Sin

In the first session of this study we identified the "sin thing." Now we are going to go after it, identifying some of the very common and acceptable sins and calling them what they are. We need to hear God's voice on this "sin thing" and accept His strength to fight back. In this session we will seek to let the light of God's Word and Spirit shine on our lives and reveal the reality of sin. Then we will seek to walk away from the darkness and toward the light.

Knowing and Being Known

Read 1 John 3:4–10

2. According to John, how does God feel about sin in the life of a Christian?

What would John say to Christians who feel discouraged and who are convinced they cannot overcome sinful patterns in their lives?

What would John say to Christians who have justified sinful behaviors in their lives by saying, "It's not a really big or bad sin—I'm sure God doesn't mind."

3. John often speaks in dualisms (dramatic contrasts). What contrast does John draw between the following:

- The work of God and the work of the Devil

- The children of God and the children of the Devil

The Poison of Pride

Have you ever gone on a diet, and then you walk into a restaurant and find yourself amazed by the garbage others will put into their bodies? You look around and wonder, What is wrong with these people? Have they no self-control? Do they have no moral power or strength of will? How can they just cram this kind of junk into their bodies? Is there no moral fiber or character in this entire restaurant?

You entertain all of these questions in spite of the fact that you were eating the same junk three days ago and you will probably be eating it again in about a week. I don't know if you have been there, but I sure have! Because you are temporarily saying no to these things, you can develop a sense of superiority.

Here are a few symptoms you can look for to see if pride has a grip on you:

- You notice that others are just not as spiritual as you. They don't practice the spiritual disciplines and exercise them as often or as long as you do.
- You discover that you enjoy passing judgment on others.
- You keep track of how often you pray and how much you read the Bible, and you give yourself a little gold star for your good behavior.

The Subtle Sin of Selfishness

Once at a pastors' conference I asked if anyone had ever had a church member complain about music. Every person in that room raised their hands and started to laugh. They went on to tell some horror stories about battles fought over songs and styles.

Now think about this for a moment. We sing about God's greatness. We lift our voices and declare our need to take up the cross and follow Jesus. And then people say, "We are not singing about the need to take up the cross and die to self with the tune I like, so I'm going to leave and go take up my cross where they sing the tunes I like."

We can try to disguise these attitudes with all kinds of flowery language, but it is really just plain old-fashioned selfishness.

Read Ecclesiastes 7:16 and Matthew 23:1–12

4. How did Jesus feel about pride and overrighteousness in the lives of religious people?

What is the antidote for the sickness of pride?

5. How have you seen pride and overrighteousness creep into your heart and attitudes?

How does a proper understanding of yourself as a servant to others help destroy the grip of pride?

Read Philippians 2:1–5

6. According to the apostle Paul (Philippians 2:2–4), what kind of attitudes and actions should mark the lives of followers of Christ?

   How does this fly in the face of a culture that nurtures and even encourages selfishness?

7. How does the model of Jesus' life (Philippians 2:5) call you to actions of service rather than a life of selfishness?

Partiality

Do you give undivided attention and full charm to those who have high status, wealth, or charisma? Do you ever see a person who can be useful to you or offer you something, so you give him or her special attention? You look him directly in the eyes, smile, agree with what he says, and do all you can to make him like you. Have you ever been there?

Have you ever met a person who did not have a lot to offer and found yourself suddenly disinterested? This person didn't have a lot of money, was not particularly attractive, and had little influence, so you didn't give him or her much attention. We hate to admit it, but we can all be tempted toward an attitude of partiality—being more partial to certain people than others.

I was visiting a church one Sunday and was greatly distracted by a man standing behind me who was singing very loud and very badly off-key. I found myself greatly bothered that he was ruining my worship time. Eventually I glanced behind me with two things in mind. First, I wanted to know who was distracting me, and second, I hoped he would notice my glance and stop being so intrusive.

As I looked back, I saw a young man who was obviously severely mentally disabled. His face was full of the joy of God. With utter abandonment he was pouring his spirit out to the God who loved him.

At that moment I saw the sin in my own heart.

What is one selfish attitude or action you need to surrender to God?

Read James 2:1–4

8. What are some of the common forms of partiality that exist in our world and in the church today?

9. What can you do to help create a more embracing and loving atmosphere in one of these places:

    • In your home
    • In your church
    • In your workplace
    • In a social setting

Read Philippians 4:4–7

10. The apostle Paul was serving time in jail because he had been faithful as a follower of Christ. While there he wrote a letter to the Philippian Christians. What do you learn from Paul's attitude of joy and thankfulness in the middle of a tough situation?

Failure to Be Grateful

A number of years ago a family I know well had an experience that reminds me of the human capacity to be ungrateful. It was snack time, and the two young boys were upstairs waiting for Mom to bring the snacks ... because this was her job! As she was bringing the boys their snack, she fell and injured her ankle rather badly. There she lay on the floor with snack in hand.

She did not want to concern her younger sons, so she remained silent as she tried to get up on an ankle that did not want to support her. Then one of them yelled, "Mom, where is the snack?" She called back, "Honey, Mommy can't bring it right this second, because I've fallen and hurt my ankle." One of her sons yelled back, "Well, can't you just crawl up?"

Ingratitude is real obvious in kids, but there is a lot of the "Can't you just crawl up" attitude in all of us. "Can't I have what I want when I want it? If I can't, I won't be a happy camper! I'll fuss and complain!" So often our gratitude is tied to our circumstances.

11. What is one deep joy you are experiencing in your life right now, and what are you doing to express gratitude to God?

Celebrating and Being Celebrated

Pray together and lift up words of gratitude to God for what He has done for you as individuals and as a group. You might want to use some of the following categories to guide your time of prayer:

- Thanksgiving for the way your life and faith have been enriched through your relationship with group members.
- Thanks for family members.
- Gratitude for the material things God provides for you.
- Thanksgiving for spiritual growth you have experienced through the Spirit's presence in your life.
- Any other joys you feel moved to express.

Loving and Being Loved

In this session you read about the conflict that can exist in churches over musical styles and song choices. Sadly, there is almost a universal reality that conflicts can arise over selfishness in this area. Commit as a group to make it your goal to affirm, encourage, and bless as many people as you can in your church music program. Go as a group, or on your own, and thank your church music director, vocalists, instrumentalists, and the technical team that helps bring your worship music alive. Pour out God's love for these faithful servants who often serve week after week without getting affirmed and encouraged.

Serving and Being Served

Every church has certain tasks that need to be done that most people avoid. They are almost always done in secret by staff or volunteers who love God and see their service as an offering to God. Pair up with one of your small group members, contact one of these faithful, unnoticed workers, ask them to train you in their task, and then give them a day off. This will give you a greater appreciation for their service, as well as give them a little break.

Love One Another

I JOHN 2:7–17; 4:7–12

An author named Robert Roberts writes about a family ther-
apist named Jim Roberts who had an amazing experience
while visiting the fourth-grade class of his son.

The teacher had organized a balloon stomp. A balloon
stomp is when every child in the class has a piece of string tied
to their ankles with a balloon connected at the end of the
string. The object of a balloon stomp is to obliterate everyone
else's balloon without letting anything happen to your balloon.
It was everybody for himself and each against all. As soon as
you were stomped and your balloon was popped, you were out
and you had to sit down. The child who still had an intact balloon when everyone else's was shredded was the winner.

The teacher gave the signal and the children leapt fero-
ciously on each other's balloons while trying to protect their
own. All, that is, except one or two who lacked the spirit of
competition. They were just dismayed by all the hullabaloo
and their balloons were soon laid waste. In a few seconds, all
the balloons were burst but one . . . the winner.

Later, a class of mentally impaired children was brought in
and prepared to play the same game. Balloons were tied to
their ankles and they were briefed on the rules of play. Said
Roberts, "I got a sinking feeling in my midsection. I wanted to
spare those kids the brawl that was about to take place."

They had only the foggiest notion of what this was all
about. After a few moments of confusion, the idea got across
to one or two of them that balloons were supposed to be
stomped, and gradually it caught on. But as the game got
under way, it was clear that these kids missed the spirit of it.

They went about methodically, intentionally, getting their
balloons stomped. One girl carefully held her own balloon in

41

place so that a boy could pop it, and then he did the same for her. When all the balloons were gone, the entire class cheered in unison.

These children, Roberts said, had mistaken this brawl for an exercise in community. In the original game, only one child could win, and the rest were relegated to the place of loser. But these children discovered a way to make everyone a winner. In normal balloon stomping the participants are alienated from each other. It's you against me. But as these children played it, the game became an occasion for love. Instead of feeling anxious about the other players, there was a sense of partnership. The play of these children seemed to foster generosity, trust, cooperation, gentleness, and concern for one another. And you have to ask yourself the question, Who got the game right?

Making the Connection

1. Describe some of the "balloon stomping" you see in one of these places:

   - In your home
   - In the workplace
   - In social settings
   - In the church

Why are we so prone to play the balloon-stomping game?

Knowing and Being Known

Read 1 John 2:7–11

2. What are signs that people are walking in the darkness?

What are signs that they are walking in the light?

Love in Action

In a large church in South America, a pastor got up to bring the message. He stood before the congregation and said, "Love one another," then he sat down. Everyone just sat there and stared at him and then at each other. No one knew what to do.

A few moments later he stood up, took his place behind the podium, and said, "Love one another," and he took his seat again. Once more the congregation sat in stunned silence ... maybe thinking, *That's kind of a short message.*

He stood up a third time and said, "Love one another," and he sat down. Then a few people caught on to the rules of the game. They turned to the people around them and said, "How are you doing? Can I pray for you? Is there some area of life where you could use some help? Could I offer you some encouragement?" They began to extend love to each other right then and there!

That day a congregation heard the commandment of God in a whole new way!

3. How has one of your relationships changed since you became a follower of Christ and started walking in the light?

Describe a relationship that still needs transformation as you learn to live more and more in God's light.

4. What is one relationship where you have a hard time expressing love?

How can your small group members pray for you as you seek a tender heart and loving spirit toward this person?

What actions could you take that would begin to express love toward this person?

Read 1 John 2:12–14

5. Read verses 12–14 *not* as if they were written to three different age-groups, or maturity levels, but to all followers of Christ at different points in their journey of faith. What does John say about us as Christ followers?

How does confidence of these truths empower you to be a person of love?

6. Describe how you are experiencing one of these truths in a deep and personal way in your life right now.

How would you like to grow deeper in your understanding of one of the truths presented by John in this passage?

The Lure of the World

The problem we face today needs very little time for its statement. Our lives in a modern city grow too complex and overcrowded. Even the necessary obligations which we feel we must meet grow like Jack's beanstalk, and before we know it we are bowed down with burdens, crushed under committees, strained, breathless, and hurried, panting through a never ending program of appointments.

—Thomas R. Kelly, *A Testament of Devotion* (Harper & Row, 1941)

Read 1 John 2:15–17

7. How would John describe a person who is in love with the world?

8. What is one hint or sign you have learned to identify in your own life when you start to fall in love with the world?

What do you do to cut off this enticement to love the world and turn your attention back to the things of God?

I Love You "in the Lord"

Years ago I served in a church where I learned a lasting lesson about love. There was a couple who had been in the church their whole lives, but there was not much love in them that I could see. They complained about young people who were not as devout as they should be. They were upset about ministries that we had failed to do and others that we did do. They were vocal about their displeasure over the music in the church because we used drums and they were sure there were no drums in the Bible. They complained that my kids ran in the sanctuary, and they felt this was neither appropriate nor reverent. Then they pointed out that I did not do enough visitation.

Meeting with them was always very hurtful. But after all of their critical words they would say, "But Pastor John, we love you in the Lord."

I think that phrase gets misused in the church sometimes. If you don't like someone, don't think good thoughts about them, don't want what is best for them, don't believe the best about them, and don't act in a loving way toward them, then is it right to say that you are "loving them in the Lord"?

Loving someone in the Lord is not a lower kind of love. It is not a spiritual tolerating of someone you really can't stand. It is actually the *highest* form of love!

Read 1 John 4:7–12

9. Imagine that the apostle John comes face-to-face with the couple described in the story above. What would he say to them about how to love someone in the Lord?

10. We all receive love in different ways. What is one way people can clearly show you that they love you with the love of God?

11. How does focusing on the sacrifice of Jesus Christ for your sins help you grow in your ability to love others?

What is one act of love you could show to another person in the coming week?

Celebrating and Being Celebrated

John is clear that all love begins with God:

This is how God showed his love among us: He sent his one and only Son into the world that we might live through him. This is love: not that we loved God, but that he loved us and sent his Son as an atoning sacrifice for our sins.

(1 John 4:9–10)

The beginning is God's initiative, the middle is God's persevering passion for us, the end of life is wrapped in God's consuming love.

Take time as a small group and lift up prayers of praise for God's unfailing love for you. Celebrate His love for you at these different times of your lives:

- When you were still in your mother's womb (Psalm 139:13)
- When you were still rebellious and running from him (Romans 5:8)
- When you were facing hard times (Romans 8:36–39)

Loving and Being Loved

It is easy to be loving toward those who love us. It is hard to show extravagant love toward those who tend to be negative and complainers. Do this very carefully and tenderly, but think of one person you know who tends to think he or she "loves people in the Lord" but actually is negative toward them. Seek to do two things over the coming month:

1. Pray for this person's heart to grow tender through the work of the Spirit.
2. Look for opportunities to give verbal affirmation to this person. This must be authentic, so look for whatever good you can see and speak words of blessing.

Allow God to touch and make this person tender through the love of God being extended through you.

Serving and Being Served

We all have people in our lives who have functioned as conduits of God's love. They have experienced the endless ocean of the love of God, and it has poured through their lives into ours. Take time in the coming week to write them a note or give them a small gift expressing how you have been touched by the way God's love has filled your life because of them. Put this in writing so they can keep the letter and go back to it when they need to be reminded that God has used them in wonderful ways.

Living as Children of God

I JOHN 2:29–3:10; 5:18–21

One of the great human quests throughout history has been trying to find the right name to use for God. What kind of word can you use to describe the all-powerful, all-knowing, just, and holy Sovereign of the universe?

In the Bible God is given many names. He is called: Yahweh (Lord), I AM WHO I AM, Adonai (Lord), Elohim (The God of the Hosts), and El Shaddai (God Almighty), just to name a few. Each of these names captures a portion of God's character.

We look for images and adjectives that could express His greatness. Rock, shield, fortress, and king are a few efforts to define the indefinable majesty of our God.

Every generation seeks to find the right words to express their worship of the living God. Some time ago our kids were in a group singing, "Our God Is an Awesome God." The song leaders had the kids replace the word *awesome* with their adjective of choice, any word that would help them describe God. Our kids came home singing, "Our God is a tubular God." We were not entirely sure what this meant and we knew that some people might not find this wording appropriately reverent, but to our kids, *tubular* expressed the awe, wonder, and joy they felt for God.

One day, almost two thousand years ago, a Jewish carpenter used a word that no one had ever thought of using for God. He used an old word, a nursery word, a word that little infants would use to address their father. The word was *Abba*. This was a very tender and intimate word, kind of like *daddy*. It was often the first word a little Jewish boy or girl would speak, because it was easy to pronounce. One day Jesus turned His eyes heavenward and addressed God as His Abba.

In all of recorded history, no one had ever thought of speaking to God in this way. Jesus spoke this word for the very first time. He lived His life in a new way—as Abba's child. So Abba was often on His lips and always on His heart.

Making the Connection

1. What is one name for God that you like to use, and why does it help express your heart toward God?

    What is one adjective you like to use to express the character and nature of God?

    How have you experienced this attribute of God?

Knowing and Being Known

Read I John 2:28–3:3

2. John points to one of the most extravagant gifts God has given—the right for us to become children of God (3:1)! What does it mean to see yourself as a child of God?

Abba Is Enough

Jesus had a profound sense of what it meant to be Abba's child. He modeled for us what it means to live our lives as children of God. One day Satan came to Jesus and made a series of offers. "Why don't You turn these stones into bread? You will be a satisfied man. Why don't You throw yourself down from a high place? The angels will protect You, and You will be an impressive man. Why don't You fall down and worship me? I will give You governments and multinational corporations, and You will be a success." The Devil seemed to be offering everything a person could want and more!

Jesus said no to it all! Jesus lived with a deep and profound sense that He was Abba's child. And for Jesus, that was enough. He didn't need to be impressive, successful, or famous. Jesus had a satisfaction that the Devil could never understand. It was like Jesus was saying to the Enemy, "What you are offering does not begin to touch the value of what I have as Abba's child."

The things the Devil offered were like trash compared to what Jesus had as Abba's child. The same is true today. All the Enemy might offer you or me, no matter how good it might look at that moment, is like garbage compared to what we receive as a child of God.

You Are Abba's Child

Not only did Jesus see Himself as Abba's child, but He said that we can call God by this same intimate name. You and I, ordinary people, can know that God is a Father who is tenderly devoted to us. Jesus said, "You can be Abba's child."

Those who are led by the Spirit of God are sons of God. For you did not receive a spirit that makes you a slave again to fear, but you received the Spirit of sonship. And by him we cry, "Abba, Father." The Spirit himself testifies with our spirit that we are God's children. Now if we are children, then we are heirs—heirs of God and co-heirs with Christ, if indeed we share in his sufferings in order that we may also share in his glory.

(Romans 8:14–17)

But when the time had fully come, God sent his Son, born of a woman, born under law, to redeem those under law, that we might receive the full rights of sons. Because you are sons, God sent the Spirit of his Son into our hearts, the Spirit who calls out, "Abba, Father." So you are no longer a slave, but a son; and since you are a son, God has made you also an heir.

(Galatians 4:4–7)

3. As a follower of Christ, God is your Abba. How does this reality impact how you see one of the following:

- God
- Yourself
- Other followers of Christ
- Seekers

4. Describe a time when you felt a deep sense of connectedness with God as your Abba.

5. What kind of attitude should a child of God have when he or she draws near to the Father (1 John 2:28 and Romans 8:14–17)?

   How does this reflect on the way you approach God?

6. What are some of the contrasts between being a hired servant and a beloved child?

   How are you growing in your understanding of yourself as God's beloved son or daughter?

The Father Is Fond of You!

There was a priest from Detroit named Edward Farrel who went on his two-week summer vacation to Ireland. His one living uncle was about to celebrate his eightieth birthday. On the great day the priest and his uncle got up before dawn and dressed in silence. They took a walk along the shores of Lake Killarney. Standing side by side, with not a word exchanged, and staring straight at the rising sun, suddenly the uncle turned and went skipping down the road. He was radiant, beaming, smiling from ear to ear. His nephew said, "Uncle Shamis, you really look happy." "I am lad." "Want to tell me why?" His eighty-year-old uncle replied, "Yes, you see, me Abba is very fond of me."

—Brennan Manning, *Abba's Child* (NavPress, 1994)

7. If God, your Abba, could sit face-to-face with you right now, what words of love would He speak to you?

Read I John 5:18–21

8. As John draws to the close of this letter, he draws out some implications for children of God. What does John teach about your relationship to *one* of the following:

   • Sin
   • The Devil
   • God

9. If Abba is Father to all followers of Christ, this makes us brothers and sisters. How have you experienced family love among the community of God's people?

10. As Abba's child, what is one area of sin the Father is calling you to leave behind as you follow Him?

How can your small group members encourage and challenge you to surrender this area of sin to the Father's hands?

11. Describe a time when you experienced God's protective fatherly hand keeping you safe.

Celebrating and Being Celebrated

As Abba, God has done so much for each of us. Take time to pray together as a small group and celebrate some of the things God has done for you. Celebrate His fatherly provision, protection, and discipline. Also, praise Him for giving you His name and calling you His own. You might also want to give thanks for the inheritance you have as His heir. What we have today does not begin to compare with all that the Father has in store for us! Celebrate His goodness.

Loving and Being Loved

If God is our Abba, our loving Father, then we are brothers and sisters with all followers of Christ. We need to beware of petty sibling rivalries and anything that might cause strife and division in the family.

If you have a strained relationship with another follower of Christ, tell your small group about it. You don't need to use a name, only the situation. You might want to talk about this with only one or two members, or the whole group. Invite them to pray for you and to keep you accountable to seek restoration and healing in this relationship. Seek to restore love where it has been lost or strained.

Serving and Being Served

Commit to serve other followers of Christ by reminding them that they are Abba's children. Write a note or send an e-mail with the express intention of heightening their awareness that they are God's beloved children. You might want to include the Romans 8 and Galatians 4 passages. Commit as a group to lavish other Christ followers with reminders of His fatherly love.

Free to Love

I JOHN 3:11–18, 5:1–5

One day, while sitting on an airplane, I saw a picture of our world. I was sitting in the front row of my section. Directly in front of me was another section of the plane. The people in that section sat in bigger seats, they ate nicer meals and better snacks, the flight attendants paid more attention to them, and the passengers there went by a different designation. They were called "first class." They were first-class people who got first-class seating, food, and service.

The rest of us, by contrast, were called "coach." The differences between us and the first-class people were clear to see. They ate on china; we ate off of little plastic trays. They drank from crystal; we got plastic cups. They got warm, moist towels to cleanse their pores and refresh their weary faces at the end of the trip; we had to sit in our facial sweat. There was a curtain drawn between us, an iron curtain. This piece of immovable material could not be violated. There was no question that they were in the Holy of Holies and we were in the courtyard of the Gentiles.

The first-class people even had their own restroom, to provide for the needs of all four of them. The hundreds of "cattle" in the back of the plane, myself included, had to share two restrooms. I discovered this in a very personal way when I got up to use the restroom and discovered a line of people going down the aisle of the coach section. I asked the flight attendant, "Would it be okay, since I'm seated right near the front, to use the restroom up in first class?" She said, "No. That's first class; you can't go up there."

I informed her that personal bladder control is not my strong suit, and that she might want to consider letting me use the vacant bathroom in first class. She responded essentially by saying, "Do you see this curtain? This is the border, the Berlin Wall, and I'm Checkpoint Charlie. You will not be passing through."

Making the Connection

1. How are the first-class and coach sections of an airplane a picture of our world?

    How does this mentality impact our relationships with others?

Knowing and Being Known

Read 1 John 3:11–15 and Genesis 4:1–12

2. What do we learn about Cain's actions and the condition of his heart?

Will I Embrace or Exclude?

John asks this central question, Will we be people who embrace others or exclude them? Will we take others into our hearts or shut them out?

As we have seen in our study of I John, there is a theme of dualism (clear contrasts). In this passage, the opposites are Cain and Abel. One is evil and one is righteous. There are two options, love or hate. John is showing us that hate is like murder because we sacrifice the other person for the sake of self. And love is about sacrificing for the sake of others, even those who might hate you.

What a dramatic contrast! To choose hatred is to choose death. To choose love is to choose life. Hatred and death are the spirit of the Evil One. Love and life are the kingdom of God. John lays out two alternatives, and only two. Now we have to choose which path we will walk. Ultimately, to choose love is to embrace others and to choose hate is to exclude them!

How do Cain and Abel become a picture of how hatred can poison relationships and kill love?

3. What are some common practices that exclude others and make them feel like outcasts?

Will I Give or Withhold?

The apostle John takes off the gloves, and things start to get a little messy here. We are often content to present love as a feeling or collection of platitudes. John does not play this game! He is clear that love is about giving. Think about it, the most famous verse in the Bible affirms this same view of love:

> For God so *loved* the world that he *gave* his one and only Son, that whoever believes in him shall not perish but have eternal life. (John 3:16, emphasis added)

God's love was evidenced by giving and not withholding.

In the same way, we are called to a love that leads to action. When we see a need, we can't withhold but need to give, and do so generously and willingly. We need to ask ourselves if we are showing love through what we give to others and God.

Identify one such action in your life and how you can battle against this.

4. What are behaviors or actions that will create a climate of embracing love?

What can you do to create more of a loving and embracing atmosphere in one of these places:

- *In your home*
- *In your small group*
- *In your church*
- *In your workplace*

Read 1 John 3:16–18

5. What has God given as evidence of His love for you?

What does God call us to give if we truly love others?

6. What are ways we can show love with our words, and how can we confirm these words with actions?

Loving words:	Actions that confirm our love:

7. What is one need you are aware of that you can meet, thereby living out the love of Jesus Christ?

It is critical that we begin our pursuit of love with an intimate and authentic relationship with God. We can't simply work at being more loving toward God and others and expect to succeed. The foundation for all love is a healthy and growing relationship with God through Jesus Christ.

Read 1 John 5:1–5

8. John wants us to know the source and strength of our love. According to John, how do we develop a heart of love for others?

How do we develop a heart that is deeper in love with God?

What is the source of our power to overcome this world?

9. What are you doing in your life right now to develop and deepen your love for God?

A Foundation for Love

The practice of godliness is an exercise or discipline that focuses upon God. From this Godward attitude arise the character and conduct that we usually think of as godliness. So often we try to develop Christian character and conduct without taking the time to develop God-centered devotion. We try to please God without taking the time to walk with Him and develop a relationship with Him. This is impossible to do. . . .

Now it is obvious that such a God-centered lifestyle cannot be fully developed and maintained apart from the solid foundation of devotion to God. Only a strong personal relationship with the living God can keep such a commitment from becoming oppressive and legalistic. John writes that God's commands are not burdensome; a godly life is not wearisome, but this is true only because a godly person is first of all devoted to God.

—Jerry Bridges, *The Practice of Godliness* (InterVarsity Press, 1983)

How does this help you become a more passionate lover of people?

10. What is one of God's commands that you are struggling to obey?

How can your small group members pray for you as you seek to joyfully follow God's command for you in this area of your life?

Celebrating and Being Celebrated

Pray together and celebrate the brothers and sisters God has placed in your life who have shown you love and who have embraced you. These could be siblings by birth, or they could be brothers and sisters in faith. Praise God for their lives and for how He has shown you love and care through their lives.

Loving and Being Loved

In the first sidebar in session four of this study, you read about a pastor in a South American church who preached a very short, but powerful, sermon. His sermon was, "Love each other." Take ten minutes as a group right now to express love to each other. Let the Spirit guide you to needs or prayer concerns.

Serving and Being Served

John calls us to open our eyes to the needs around us and to respond through loving service. The example he uses is financial. When we see a person who lacks the material needs of life, we should help provide what they need.

Have one of your group members research local ministries (maybe in your own church) that provide food and clothes for those in need. Consider agreeing as a group to make it a habit that when you go grocery shopping, you will buy an item to donate to this organization or ministry. Don't give the old stuff you have in your cabinet that no one wants to eat. Pick the best items that you and your family would want. Also consider buying some clothing items to donate as well.

Deliver these clothes and food items to the organization you have chosen. Consider making this part of your lifestyle, not just a one-time project.

Session One — It's a Sin Thing
I JOHN 1:5–2:2

Question 1

In this session we are going to deal with sin. So you will need to invite the members of your group to lower their defenses and allow the Spirit to work. The reality is, when we deal with sin, things can get a little messy. This is what happens during surgery. When we go after the heart of sin, some blood will be spilled.

Be sure to pray as a group for very open and responsive spirits. This is a session that some might want to avoid. No one likes to face their sin, but we all need to do it. Pray for the Spirit's work to be done in your lives as you prepare for some spiritual surgery.

Question 2

The image of light is one of the three great definitions John gives of God. In the gospel of John, chapter 4, John says that "God is Spirit." Later in 1 John 4 he says, "God is love." And here in the beginning of the first letter of John we learn that "God is light." Our God is perfect light and has no darkness in Him at all!

Light, here in John, is used as a metaphor for God's goodness. It speaks of the character of God. This same use is found often in the Old Testament:

> *The Lord is my light and my salvation—*
> *whom shall I fear?*

(Psalm 27:1)

> Your word is a lamp to my feet
> and a light for my path.

(Psalm 119:105)

John is saying that God is sheerly good—unmixed, untainted goodness. Then John draws a conclusion. Because God is light, as His followers, we must walk in the light. This is a kind of metaphor. We are to live lives that are sheerly good. We are to live lives of moral beauty. We are to live lives that overflow with truth and love. This is what it means for followers of Christ to walk in the light.

As a group you may have talked of many other properties of light that parallel how God works in the life of a follower of Christ: illumination, warmth, and other parallels might have been mentioned. In other passages, the image of light is used in other ways, but in this passage, what John seems to be getting at is the pure moral beauty of God and the invitation for every follower of Christ to walk in this same spirit of truth and love.

However, there were false teachers in the days of John, and their words and teachings were clearly at odds with their moral character. They were speaking and holding up one standard, but their lives told an entirely different story. John was deeply concerned about this. He wanted all the followers of Christ to be able to identify the false claims of these deceptive teachers. Some of them had actually left the fellowship, but they were still trying to poison the thinking of the church members by feeding them false teachings about what it meant to be a follower of Christ.

Questions 3–4

The first false claim being made was this: some were claiming to walk with God and have intimate fellowship with Him, while they were actually walking in the darkness. They had lives of moral depravity. Their hearts and actions were far from God. This radically contradictory life was a sign that they did not really understand the gravity of sin or the truth of grace.

The implications of this false claim and understanding of sin is that people become liars and don't walk according to the truth. We can boast that we are alive spiritually, but if our lives are filled with darkness, our words are a lie.

John corrected this false understanding by teaching that we are to walk in the light even as He is in the light. Claiming to be in the light is not enough. We need to walk in the light. Our lives should reflect the moral beauty of the God we follow.

John's message for the followers of Christ is that if we walk in the light, we will have true fellowship and community with each other. And the blood Jesus shed on the cross will cleanse us, purify us, and take away all of our sin. We become forgiven people.

Questions 5–7

The second false claim being made was this: Some were boasting that they were free from the guilt of sin. They claimed that they were free from any guilt or judgment of sin and that they had attained this on their own, with no help from Jesus.

The implications of this false claim and understanding of sin is that we deceive ourselves. Not only do we lie to others, but we are living with the wool pulled over our own eyes! We are deceiving ourselves and proving that God's truth is not alive in us.

John corrected this false understanding by teaching that followers of Christ need to confess their sins. We need to acknowledge the reality that we are sinful. Denial does not remove sin; only confession can do this.

John's message for the followers of Christ is that the God who is completely reliable and just will extend us His forgiveness and cleanse us from all of our wrongdoings. When we deny our sin, it continues to cling to our soul. When we admit our sinfulness, we can experience cleansing and wholeness.

Question 8

The third false claim being made was this: Some claimed that they were free of sin and morally spotless. They did not need Jesus or anyone else to declare them clean; they were claiming absolute moral purity all on their own. They believed they did not need forgiveness because they had never done anything wrong.

This false claim about sin makes God out to be a liar. You see, all through the history of God's people, God was clear to communicate that all people have sinned. Therefore, to claim personal moral purity was to claim that God was lying about the condition of all people as sinners. This also proved that God's Word was not in them, because the Word of God is replete with teaching about the sinful nature of the human heart.

John corrected this false understanding by reminding us that we are all sinners. The words, "if anyone does sin" are best translated, "when anybody sins" or "when you sin." The correction is that we *all* sin! John does not teach this to depress or discourage us, but so that we can take a good look at the truth. Once we realize we are all sinful, we can see our need to receive God's gift of grace.

John's message for the followers of Christ is truly astonishing! When we fall into sin, we can live with an assurance that we have an advocate who stands in the very presence of God on our behalf. His name is Jesus Christ. He is the One who is just, true, and righteous. He laid down His life as a sacrifice to pay the price for us. And He did this not just for us, but also for every person on the face of the earth. His desire is that we will acknowledge our sin and look to Him for forgiveness.

Session Two — Experiencing God's Forgiveness
I JOHN 1:8–2:6

Question 1

Do you know anyone who has been pulled over and openly admitted, "I was speeding! I've been caught red-handed. I am guilty! I deserve punishment! Please bring the full extent of the law to bear against me for my crime!" Of course not. When we get caught, we all want grace!

We need to learn how to confess in a way that leads to growth and health. We need to learn how to express our heartfelt confession in a way that will help us experience and live in God's grace. We must learn from the past and still walk forward and continue growing in Christlikeness.

Some people live their lives with a sense that they have to inflict a certain measure of pain on themselves to pay for their sins. It is as if God's grace is not enough. They need to add their own punishment and penance to God's grace.

When I was growing up I had a dog that would run off into a corner and lay there with its tail between its legs when it would do something wrong. After a certain amount of time my dog would come back and everything would be fine again. Many of us are like that. We can feel like there is a certain amount of time that must transpire and some type of punishment that needs to be inflicted before we can come back into God's presence. Once the timer goes off, our spiritual time-out is over, and we can enter God's presence again.

This is not God's plan for us. He wants us to experience the wonderful healing and freedom that comes through confession. He longs for us to know His grace in new and deep ways.

Questions 2–3

We need to make a distinction between positional forgiveness and relational forgiveness. As a Christian, my position, my status before God is as one saved by grace. I can have absolute trust in God's graciousness. I don't have to worry: *What if I go to sleep after committing a sin and I don't get a chance to confess it before I die.* My position is as one who is utterly forgiven by God . . . past, present, and future!

The reality is, we are in an ongoing relationship with God. Sin blocks intimacy anytime it gets into a relationship. As in the case with any relationship, when sin has damaged it, there needs to be confession and repentance for reconciliation to take place. We can put it this way, confession is demanded of followers of Christ not so much because God needs it in order to forgive, but rather that we need it to heal and be changed.

At the heart of it, confession involves owning appropriate responsibility for what we have done.

Questions 4–5

We need to learn how to see the cost and consequences of all sins: anger, lust, gossip, jealousy, deception . . . you name it. We need to see through the eyes of the person we have sinned against and also through the eyes of God.

There are two key questions we need to ask when confessing a sin.

1. Why did I do it?

This is about getting to the core of our own motives! We need to honestly say, "I lied to cover up my own poor behavior or to avoid getting into trouble." Or, "I gossiped about this person because I was jealous and felt hurt and insignificant." When we learn to identify our motives, it helps us confess more specifically and honestly.

2. What was the result of my sinful actions?

This is about learning not to candy-coat the cost of our sins. We must be brutally honest and say, "I lied and now I feel guilty." Or, "Now there is a breach in my relationship with this person and I feel distant from God." We must admit that now we are more likely to commit this sin again. When we say, "I have hurt God, I have damaged another person, I have ruined my reputation, or I have shamed the name of Christ," we are woken up to the reality that sin always costs us!

When we do this, we begin to learn. It is a sign of spiritual growth. As we humbly see our own sinfulness, we become far less judgmental. All of a sudden our eyes are on the cross and not busy scrutinizing the lives of others.

This is not about beating ourselves up. It is about being honest about the consequences of our sins and admitting our need for the overflowing grace of God.

Questions 6–7

I used to think of these as pretty depressing verses. Just the opposite is true. They are a great gift to followers of Christ. Many wise writers about the spiritual life have written that when we begin praying confession, but feel a dryness and apathy, it is appropriate to ask for the gift of tears. These tears are to help us experience the pain of others and the pain of God.

When our hearts are working right, when we confess how we have hurt others, it should go deep into our heart. In some way, on some level, we should experience their pain.

There also needs to be a balancing statement here for those who tend to beat themselves up. We need to remember that confession is an act of grace and can only be done safely in the context of grace. There are those who not only quickly and forcefully take full responsibility for their own sins, but they enthusiastically take responsibility for everyone else's sin as well.

These are the people who tend to take the blame for everything. If you are like this, you need to lean heavily into grace. You need to remind yourself that forgiveness is not based on the adequacy of your confession, but on God's loving faithfulness.

Questions 8–9

A good football team will gather following a game they have lost and study the film, play by play. They want to identify their mistakes and be sure they don't repeat them in the next game. If people will spend hours in this kind of review over a football game, how much more important is reviewing our mistakes to be sure we don't continue hurting the people we love and the God who sent His Son for us?

The acid test of confession and repentance is how we answer this question: Am I about damage control or setting things right? If we are only trying to minimize the damage, often to ourselves and our reputation, we have got it all wrong. If our heart's desire is to set things right, then we are beginning to understand what true confession is about.

We can all smell a false confession. Sadly, we have heard too many, from others and ourselves.

Think of it this way: how many times in the past twenty years has a politician been forced to leave office because of misbehavior, wrongdoing, or some sort of sin? When was the last time you heard: "I have done wrong. I have disgraced my office and breached the trust of those I was called to serve. I am heartily ashamed of my behavior, and I will therefore resign and devote my efforts to setting right the wrongs I have done."

We would love to hear somebody, just once, honestly confess to what they have done wrong and then take steps to make it right.

Questions 10–11

John is clear that Jesus is the One who intercedes for us. It is not that God is reluctant to forgive and Jesus must talk Him into it. Rather, Jesus Himself, who is in intimate relationship with the

Father, is our advocate. If we have any question about God's love and the availability of grace, we just need to look at Jesus. Jesus, the One who lived, died, and rose again, is on our side.

How can we say that what Jesus does for us is deficient? Why do we choose to punish ourselves on the spiritual time-out chair as if this will add to the intercessory work of Jesus Christ? What can we add to what Jesus has done on our behalf?

Nothing!

We need to accept His grace, bathe in it, rejoice in it, and live with assurance that His grace is always enough.

Session Three — Overcoming the Sin Thing
I JOHN 3:4–10

Question 1

Subtle sin is most dangerous because it increases our capacity for self-deception.

The truth is, we are capable of any sin in the book, but if we are going to move toward the light, we need to ruthlessly examine our hearts and lives. Specifically, we need to examine ourselves in relationship to those subtle sins that have the potential to trip us up and drive us away from the light and into the darkness.

In this session we are going to look at various areas of subtle sin and ask, *Is this getting bigger or smaller in my life? Am I walking away from this, or is it getting more and more of a grip on me?* If we are honest about this process, it may very well involve some pain. But pain is not the worst thing in life. When we speak and see the truth about ourselves, we begin to take our first steps toward the light.

Question 2

Try to answer these questions in the first person, as if you are John. After reading this passage, and in light of your last study from 1 John 1, group members will have a good sense of how John feels about sin. John is not quick to excuse sin or pretend that subtle sins don't matter. He calls us to ruthless self-examination and lives that are walked in the light of God, not the darkness of the Devil. We are children of God. We are not slaves to sin. We should live with a hope and confidence that freedom from sin is not only desirable, but expected for those who walk as fully devoted followers of Christ.

Question 3

There is a battle going on! No question about it. The Devil wants to draw us into lives filled with sin. If he can seduce us to the "big sins," all the better. But if he must resort to the subtle sins that will still drive us from God and into the darkness, this is his plan as well. The Enemy wants followers of Christ to live in the dream world that they can both indulge their sinful desires and still walk in the light.

God is at war with the Devil. Jesus came to destroy the Devil's power, domain, and grip on the lives of people. God wants us walking in the light and turning from any sinful actions, even the ones that can be deemed "little" or "acceptable."

Questions 4–5

Another way of talking about pride is overrighteousness. In Ecclesiastes 7:16 we read, "Do not be overrighteous." Does this mean, don't be too loving or truthful? Obviously not! It is talking about spiritual pride. Something happens to us as we try to improve spiritually. Too often, pride can creep in, and we begin to think more of ourselves than we ought, and less of others.

Jesus did not like pride in the lives of "religious" people back in His days, and He does not like it in our hearts today. Pride is sin, and we must recognize it and root it out. One of the best ways to do this is begin serving others. Serve in secret and do the very things you might feel you are above. Take some time to read John 13:1–17, where Jesus models servanthood for us beautifully.

Questions 6–7

Jesus is the perfect model of selflessness. Paul holds Him up as our example. We are to think of the needs and desires of others as Jesus did. We are to be careful not to insist on only our own way. We are to seek a common heart and mind—Jesus modeled this reconciling spirit. In all we do, we need to look to the example of Jesus.

Selfish attitudes will destroy friendships, erode marriages, undercut business partnerships, estrange siblings, weaken churches, and break the heart of God. We are called to self-lessness in a selfish world. Look to Jesus as you seek to turn from selfish tendencies.

Questions 8–9

When I think of that young man singing with all his might at that worship service, I realize that he could have been bitter, but he was full of joy. I, who had so much going for me, was so easily driven to frustration. In God's eyes, I wonder if this young man's worship might have been the most pleasing worship that God received in that service. That young man showed no bitterness but pure joy and gratitude.

Jesus said, "Whatever you did for one of the least of these brothers of mine, you did for me" (Matthew 25:40).

It was Jesus' way of saying, "Every person matters to me. Even if you see them as one who has no money, power, status, or strategic use to you, they still matter to Me! If you want to know the true state of your heart, ask yourself how you treat people like this. And if you don't treat the least of these the way you would treat Me, you had better know, it's a 'sin thing'!"

Questions 10–11

For some people, the only time they can be grateful is when they get something they want really, really bad. The general tone of their life is that they take things for granted and complain when they don't get what they want, right when they want it.

We need to wake up every morning and realize that God has given us the gift of life! If we are working and living in the kingdom right, we will be flooded with gratitude. We need to battle ingratitude and begin to be aggressively grateful.

Session Four—Love One Another

I JOHN 2:7–17; 4:7–12

Question 1

At the end of the day, John says that there are only two games. People are either balloon stompers or lovers. To the apostle John, there is no middle ground. John is always pressing us to make a decision.

Jesus said, "A new command I give you: Love one another. As I have loved you, so you must love one another. By this all men will know that you are my disciples, if you love one another" (John 13:34–35).

Jesus said to His followers, if you forget everything else, remember to love one another. All the commandments of God boil down to loving God and loving one another. In fact, our love for each other will be the evidence that God has set up His new community.

When you stop and ask yourself, "What does the church have to offer the world?" you will realize that our greatest impact will not be when we win a lot of theological arguments, build big facilities, design clever strategies, or prove how spiritual we are. Jesus said that the world will know that God has come to earth and penetrated this fallen and sinful planet when we love each other. He said the world will be filled with hope when they see how we love one another. The whole message of the Bible can be distilled down to this: Love God and love each other.

Questions 2–4

In John's day there were people who were not doing a great job of walking in the light. They were claiming to be spiritual giants. They knew a whole lot of stuff and they were telling others, "You should follow me. You should listen to me." But they failed to love. They were judgmental, they were misleading, and they were confusing people. We know from 1 John 2:19 that some of them had abandoned the community, the very people they were supposed to love.

So John is saying, I need to bring you back to square one. If you want to know what spiritual maturity is about, here it is: you need to love each other. If you say you walk in God's light, but you go on hating others, you are actually in the darkness. If you love others, you are in the light!

John is telling the church to remember that it is all about love. His message hit them where they lived, and it should hit us as well. When we walk in love, our relationships are dramatically changed. We learn to share and think of the needs of others rather than being selfish. Our sharp and hurtful words cease, and we learn to encourage and affirm others. We stop seeing people as stepping-stones for our personal advancement and love them for who God has made them to be. Our attitudes and actions begin to reflect the love and compassion of Jesus.

Questions 5–6

Some scholars feel these verses point to three different age-groups in the church. This could be the case. Others say these three categories are speaking to three levels of spiritual maturity. This could also be a helpful way to look at this passage. However, I feel a faithful way to read and understand this passage is that all of these words to followers of Christ can point to each and every one of us. Read these and see which ones speak to where you are in your life of faith right now.

Questions 7–8

If you read 1 John closely, you will quickly notice that John is always calling us to a point of decision. He uses dualism or opposites in this process. John talks of love or hate, truth or lies, light or darkness, God or the world.

John is saying, "There is a new game in town," and it is not about balloon stomping. The commandment he is referring to is found in John 13:34, "A new command I give you: Love one another. As I have loved you, so you must love one another."

John is clear that there is a profound dichotomy between loving the world and loving God. As Thomas Kelly reminds us, we are prone to get lured into the business of all the world's stuff. Even good things can become dangerous and evil when they monopolize our lives and keep us from loving God and loving others.

We need to scrutinize our lives and be sure the world has not gotten its hooks into us. Are we consumed with consumption? Do we spend all of our time and resources on satiating our own desires, or are we generous with God and others? Do we love the status and position we can attain before people, or are we learning to serve others? We need to ask tough questions and let the Spirit of God search our hearts.

Questions 9–11

Loving someone in the Lord is not some lower form of love, but it is the highest love of all. It is loving someone as Jesus would love them. This is why Jesus has called us to love others "as I have loved you."

Here is the hard truth. The couple who claimed to "love me in the Lord" but actually did not like me were not my favorite people either. I am sad to say that I did not seek to love them as I should have. The sad reality is that if they had raved about my family and me, I probably would have liked them a lot. I have stomped on my share of balloons in my day. I have failed to love others on more occasions than I would want to admit.

We all need to search our hearts and see where the darkness still remains. We are all on the way when it comes to learning to walk in love. The key is to be able to look at our lives and see that we are moving toward the light and loving more and more like Jesus loves.

Session Five – Living as Children of God
I JOHN 2:29–3:10; 5:18–21

Question 1

The Bible is filled with names for God and adjectives that help us put into words what we feel in our hearts about God. The beauty of these various descriptions is that they help us give voice to our prayers in so many different life situations. When we are feeling under attack and defenseless, He is our mighty tower, our fortress, and our deliverer. When we feel disoriented and confused, we can call on the One who is the light, the way, and the Good Shepherd. When we are in need, He is our provider and the giver of every good gift. There are count-less ways to describe the God we worship. Reflect on various names for God and descriptions of His character. Spend time appreciating God's greatness.

Questions 2–4

In this brief passage, there is a wonderful little phrase. It is hard to capture in the translation, but it is powerful. The text reads: "How great is the love the Father has lavished on us, that we should be called children of God! And that is what we are!" (1 John 3:1).

The portion that reads "and that is what we are" is only two little words in the Greek, but it means exactly what it says. We are His children! He does not say, "What a wonderful little metaphor or picture to help us get the idea." He says, "We *are* God's children."

When we realize and accept the overwhelming reality that we are Abba's beloved children, everything changes. God is no longer a distant and scary Deity, but an approachable and car-ing Father. We are no longer sinners lost in our rebellion; we are beloved children who are forgiven and accepted. Other Christians become our brothers and sisters; they are family. And seekers, those outside of the family, are potential brothers and sisters.

Questions 5–7

When we know that God is our Father, we realize that we have a special place in His heart. We are not a stranger or an out-sider; we are His daughter or son. We can enter His presence with confidence and joy, knowing we will be accepted with open arms. In a world where we can feel excluded and outcast, this is a great reality.

The All Better Book is a collection of children's responses to some of the world's problems. Children were asked, "In a world filled with billions of people, what should we do to be sure that no one is lonely?" Here are some of the children's responses:

> People should find lonely people and ask them their name and address. Then ask people who are not lonely

their name and address. When you have an even amount of each, assign lonely and not lonely people together in the newspaper.

—Colanie, age 8

If they feel they are not pretty you could say, "You are a lot prettier than someone I know who has big bulgy eyes."

—Kathline, age 9

We could get people a pet, or a husband or a wife, and take them places.

—Matt, age 8

Sing a song, stomp your feet, read a book. Sometimes I think no one loves me, so I do one of those.

—Brian, age 8

What does a human heart do when it feels unloved? Sometimes it runs from lover to lover, seeking approval. Sometimes it decides to make enough money or impress enough people to prove it is lovable. Sometimes it gets hurt and angry, and it grows cold, bitter, and small.

With billions of people in the world, someone should figure out a system where no one is lonely . . . and of course someone has. We are the beloved children of God!

Question 8

Up to this point in life, sin and the Devil have had great power in our lives. We could not shake the influence of the Enemy and the sting of sin. Now we have been set free! We are slaves no longer. We don't have to continue in sin. We can resist and live as overcomers. We are no longer under the control of the Devil, but under the loving leadership and protection of our heavenly Father.

Session Six—Free to Love
1 JOHN 3:11–18; 5:1–5

Question 1

Imagine getting on a plane and the people in first class get out of their seats, tear the curtain down, and invite people from coach to have their seats. Maybe they look for an elderly person or someone with a special need. They say, "You go sit in first class, and I can get a downgrade." If that ever happened, people would be amazed! Everyone would want to fly with an airline that had that kind of thing happening. All of a sudden the last are first, because the first have chosen to be last.

This is what Jesus has in mind for the church. We are to be a new community where people so love God and others that they can't help but put others first. There is always an embrace and never an exclusion.

Question 2

John's desire in the texts we will study in this session is to free us from the things that might stand in the way of our loving others. John wants to see us released to love God and love others. This ability to love will only come alive when we remove some of the obstacles that stand in the way.

John is contrasting a loving embrace with hateful exclusion. To drive his point home, John draws from the Old Testament. Cain becomes the contrast, the opposite, the polar antithesis of love. We are told that we are not to be like Cain, who belonged to the Evil One.

We need to remember that Cain was Adam and Eve's first child. Their only child. Then along came the second child, Abel. You might think Cain would be happy at the arrival of this new child. Now he would have a playmate, a friend, someone to run around with and tell secrets to. But he was not happy.

Brotherhood, which was intended as a gift, became the grounds for sibling rivalry and jealousy. Cain and Abel began playing the "who is most loved," "who is most valued," and "who is most righteous before God" game. This became a battleground for Cain and Abel, and it often becomes a point of contention in homes today.

God intended brotherhood to be a great blessing and a place for loving embracing. Instead it can become a battleground. The irony in this story is that Cain kills his brother over the issue of worship. One is a shepherd and the other is a farmer. Each brings from their abundance, and Abel's sacrifice is accepted by God and Cain's is not. Cain is filled with resentment and envy, so he does away with his brother. It is fair to say that differences in worship style had a part in the first murder. This should be a sober warning to those of us who might be quick to pick a fight over worship styles.

We might not have ever acted out our anger and vengeance the way Cain did, but the truth is that most of us have felt like Cain at one time or another. Our heart can be where Cain's heart was.

But Jesus has another plan for His people. We are to be a community who embraces and includes each other, not a body that is filled with hatred and exclusion. This is why John emphasizes that we know we love God when we love each other. This is the in-breaking of God's new community. John says this is proof that we have moved from death to life.

Questions 3–4

Every moment of every day we decide in a thousand ways if we are going to exclude or embrace. Are we going to welcome people or shut them out?

When you are in a small group and you know people well and are comfortable with them, it is easy to become exclusive. When you feel the Spirit calling you to reach out to someone new, someone who is not in your community, then you have to choose. When you walk into a church service, the loving community of God, and see someone sitting all alone, what will you do? It is almost always easier to just leave them alone and gravitate toward those you already know. But a heart alive with God's love wants to reach out and embrace others. When there are people around you from other races or backgrounds, and you could reach out to them or exclude them, you have to make a choice. When you have bitterness against a sister or brother, you know that God wants you to seek reconciliation. You can come up with a thousand reasons why not to do it, but you know the choice God wants you to make. Will you embrace or exclude?

Questions 5–7

When was the last time you made a truly extravagant sacrifice? God proved His love for us by giving His only Son. Salvation and cleansing for our sins are only because of the gift of His grace. On top of this, God grants us the presence of the Spirit, gifts of the Spirit, the fruit of the Spirit, the hope of heaven, and so much more! God lavishes us with His goodness.

In our church we have something called a cars ministry. When church members have a used car they no longer need, they can donate it to the church. The people in our cars ministry clean it up, give it a tune-up and a wax job, make sure it is running well, and then give it to a single mother in need of a car. This gift is a miracle of love to this woman and her family.

You might know someone in need and you have the means to send a gift that would show love. Be open to responding as the Spirit leads.

One of the most amazing statements in the New Testament is when we read of the early church:

> *All the believers were one in heart and mind. No one claimed that any of his possessions was his own, but they shared everything they had. With great power the apostles continued to testify to the resurrection of the Lord Jesus, and much grace was upon them all. There were no needy persons among them. For from time to time those who owned lands or houses sold them, brought the money from the sales and put it at the apostles' feet, and it was distributed to anyone as he had need.*

> (Acts 4:32–35)

Can you imagine this? There was not a needy person among them because they were so committed to giving and loving that all needs were met. What would a church look like if we devoted ourselves to giving and helping in such a way that all the needs were met?

Questions 8–10

John is clear that love gives birth to more love. However, the genesis of love is always God. Any love we have to give to others or to give to God originates with the love God has for us. We can't go out and try to muster up some personal power for loving. We will fall short every time. We need to accept God's lavish love and live in it. Then, out of the reservoir of His love, we can love each other.

We grow more and more in love with God when we learn to follow His commands. This is another way that John says, "Walk in the light." Following God's commands is about doing what He wants, it's about walking in His light, it's about loving God. As we follow God's commandments, we discover that the first is to love God, and the second is to love others. Love gives birth to a life of obedience, and a life of obedience to God gives birth to love! This becomes a cyclical dance of love that brings joy to the heart of God and results in overflowing love in the lives of others.

Willow Creek Association

Vision, Training, Resources for Prevailing Churches

This resource was created to serve you and to help you build a local church that prevails. It is just one of many ministry tools that are part of the Willow Creek Resources® line, published by the Willow Creek Association together with Zondervan.

The Willow Creek Association (WCA) was created in 1992 to serve a rapidly growing number of churches from across the denominational spectrum that are committed to helping unchurched people become fully devoted followers of Christ. Membership in the WCA now numbers over 10,000 Member Churches worldwide from more than ninety denominations.

The Willow Creek Association links like-minded Christian leaders with each other and with strategic vision, training, and resources in order to help them build prevailing churches designed to reach their redemptive potential. Here are some of the ways the WCA does that.

- **Prevailing Church Conference**—an annual two-and-a-half day event, held at Willow Creek Community Church in South Barrington, Illinois, to help pioneering church leaders raise up a volunteer core while discovering new and innovative ways to build prevailing churches that reach unchurched people.

- **Leadership Summit**—a once-a-year, two-and-a-half-day conference to envision and equip Christians with leadership gifts and responsibilities. Presented live at Willow Creek as well as via satellite broadcast to over sixty locations across North America, this event is designed to increase the leadership effectiveness of pastors, ministry staff, volunteer church leaders, and Christians in the marketplace.

- **Ministry-Specific Conferences**—throughout each year the WCA hosts a variety of conferences and training events—both at Willow Creek's main campus and off-site, across the U.S. and around the world—targeting church leaders in ministry-specific areas such as: evangelism, the arts, children, students, small groups, preaching and teaching, spiritual formation, spiritual gifts, raising up resources, etc.

- **Willow Creek Resources®**—to provide churches with trusted and field-tested ministry resources in such areas as leadership, evangelism, spiritual formation, spiritual gifts, small groups, stewardship, student ministry, children's ministry, the use of the arts—drama, media, contemporary music—and more. For additional information about Willow Creek Resources® call the Customer Service Center at 800-570-9812. Outside the U.S. call 847-765-0070.

- *WillowNet*—the WCA's Internet resource service, which provides access to hundreds of transcripts of Willow Creek messages, drama scripts, songs, videos, and multimedia tools. The system allows users to sort through these elements and download them for a fee. Visit us online at www.willowcreek.com.

- *WCA News*—a quarterly publication to inform you of the latest trends, resources, and information on WCA events from around the world.

- *Defining Moments*—a monthly audio journal for church leaders featuring Bill Hybels and other Christian leaders discussing probing issues to help you discover biblical principles and transferable strategies to maximize your church's redemptive potential.

- *The Exchange*—our online classified ads service to assist churches in recruiting key staff for ministry positions.

- **Member Benefits**—includes substantial discounts to WCA training events, a 20 percent discount on all Willow Creek Resources®, access to a Members-Only section on WillowNet, monthly communications, and more. Member Churches also receive special discounts and premier services through WCA's growing number of ministry partners—Select Service Providers.

For specific information about WCA membership, upcoming conferences, and other ministry services contact:

Willow Creek Association
P.O. Box 3188, Barrington, IL 60011-3188
Phone: 847-570-9812
Fax: 847-765-5046
www.willowcreek.com

Continue building your new community!
New Community Series
Bill Hybels and John Ortberg
with Kevin and Sherry Harney

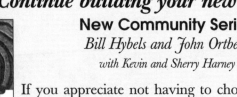

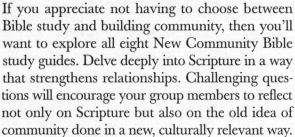

If you appreciate not having to choose between Bible study and building community, then you'll want to explore all eight New Community Bible study guides. Delve deeply into Scripture in a way that strengthens relationships. Challenging questions will encourage your group members to reflect not only on Scripture but also on the old idea of community done in a new, culturally relevant way.

Each guide contains six transforming sessions—filled with prayer, insight, intimacy, and action—to help your small group members line up their lives and relationships more closely with the Bible's model for the church.

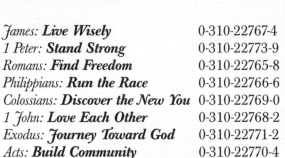

James: **Live Wisely**	0-310-22767-4
1 Peter: **Stand Strong**	0-310-22773-9
Romans: **Find Freedom**	0-310-22765-8
Philippians: **Run the Race**	0-310-22766-6
Colossians: **Discover the New You**	0-310-22769-0
1 John: **Love Each Other**	0-310-22768-2
Exodus: **Journey Toward God**	0-310-22771-2
Acts: **Build Community**	0-310-22770-4

*Look for New Community at
your local Christian bookstore.*

WILLOW
Willow Creek Resources

www.willowcreek.com

ZONDERVAN™

GRAND RAPIDS, MICHIGAN 49530 USA

WWW.ZONDERVAN.COM

Tackle the tough questions!

Tough Questions Series

Garry Poole and Judson Poling
Foreword by Lee Strobel

Tough questions. Reasonable questions. The kinds of questions that require informed and satisfying answers to challenges against the Christian faith.

Each guide within the Tough Questions series spends six sessions dealing frankly with a specific question seekers and believers often ask about Christianity. These thought-provoking discussions will help your group find answers and discover how reasonable the Christian faith really is.

How Does Anyone Know God Exists?
0-310-24502-8

What Difference Does Jesus Make?
0-310-24503-6

How Reliable Is the Bible?
0-310-24504-4

How Could God Allow Suffering and Evil?
0-310-24505-2

Don't All Religions Lead to God?
0-310-24506-0

Do Science and the Bible Conflict?
0-310-24507-X

Why Become a Christian?
0-310-24508-7

Tough Questions Leader's Guide
0-310-24509-5

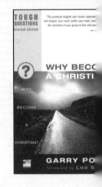

LOOK FOR Tough Questions Series
AT YOUR LOCAL CHRISTIAN BOOKSTORE.

WILLOW
Willow Creek Resources

www.willowcreek.com

ZONDERVAN™

GRAND RAPIDS, MICHIGAN 49530 USA

WWW.ZONDERVAN.COM

Walk with God Together
Walking With God Series
Don Cousins and Judson Poling

This series of six guides (and two leader's guides) provides a solid, biblical program of study for all of the small groups in your church. The Walking With God Series is designed to help lead new and young believers into a deeper personal intimacy with God, while at the same time building a strong foundation in the faith for all believers, regardless of their level of maturity. These guides are also appropriate for individual study. Titles in the series are:

Friendship with God: Developing Intimacy with God	0-310-59143-0
The Incomparable Jesus: Experiencing the Power of Christ	0-310-59153-8
"Follow Me!": Walking with Jesus in Everyday Life	0-310-59163-5
Leader's Guide 1 (covers these first three books)	0-310-59203-8
Discovering Your Church: Becoming Part of God's New Community	0-310-59173-2
Building Your Church: Using Your Gifts, Time, and Resources	0-310-59183-X
Impacting Your World: Becoming a Person of Influence	0-310-59193-7
Leader's Guide 2 (covers these last three books)	0-310-59213-5
Also available: *Walking With God Journal*	0-310-91642-9

Look for the Walking With God Series
at your local Christian bookstore.

WILLOW
Willow Creek Resources

www.willowcreek.com

GRAND RAPIDS, MICHIGAN 49530 USA

WWW.ZONDERVAN.COM